SUPERSTITION MOUNTAIN PHOTOS AND POINTS OF INTEREST

MITCHELL WAITE

CONTENTS

CHAPTER 1: SUPERSTITION MOUNTAIN

There is a difference between the Superstition Mountain and the Superstition Mountains. When speaking of Superstition Mountain, the reference is the main bluff of mountain that can be seed from the metro Phoenis area as seen below.

The Superstition Mountain is what most people see from the Valley of the Sun. It seems to fool people into thinking the Superstition Mountain range is not all that big or dangerous.   When, in fact; they are only looking at the tip of the ice burg.

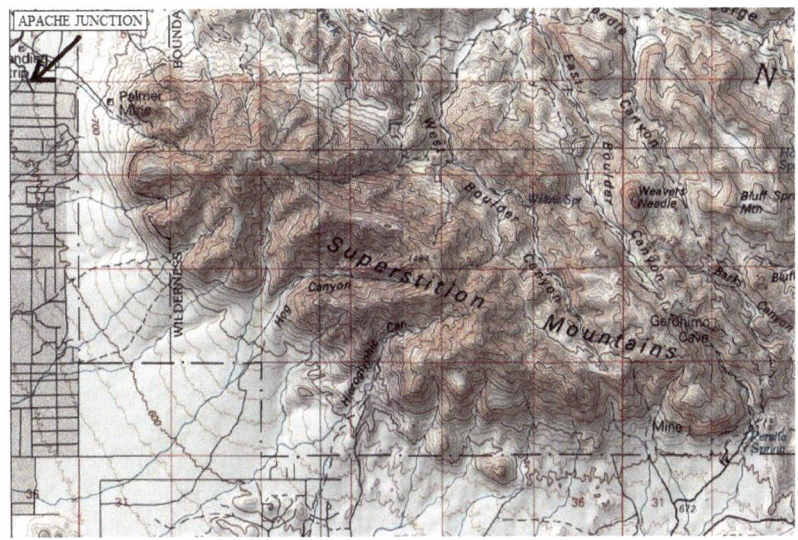

Speaking of the Superstition Mountains, the reference is to the Superstiton Mountain Range which encompasses the entire Wilderness Area. The boundry on the east side is Roosevelt Lake, west side is Apache Junction, north side are the Salt River lakes, and the south side is bound by US 60

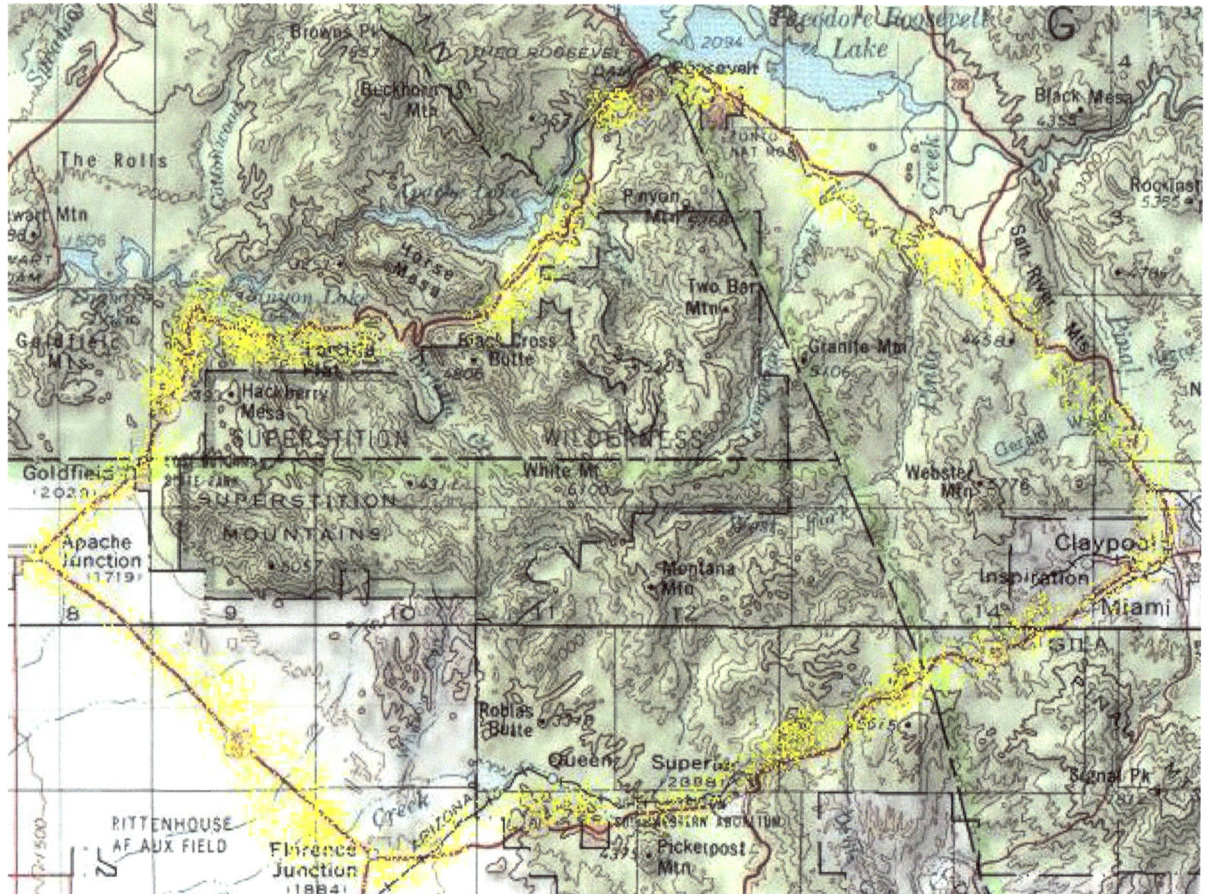

THE SUPERSTITION MOUNTAIN RANGE

The Superstition Mountains are best known for its secrets of the Lost Dutchman Gold Mine. This is the mother-lode of all lost mines. A German immagrant known as Jacob Waltz followed the gold strikes across the United States back in the late 1800's and finally settled in the new town of Phoenix, Arizona. It is here he homesteaded 160 acres of land, grew chicken for their eggs, and lived in an adobe hut. During the cooler months of the year, Jacob started prospecting for gold in the hills surounding Phoenix. He eventually ended up in the Superstition Mountains and discovering a fabously rich gold mine. He started to bring the gold out, and soon found he was being followed each time he tried to return to his mine. He was always able to elude his followers. Eventually, Jacob got sick and died. He was buried in Phoenix. For more information read "The Continuing Search for the Lost Dutchman's Gold Mine."

Starting on the west side of the Superstition Mountains there are several points of interest to visit. On the left side of the photo below, where the sheer ciffs meet the sloping foothills is a place known as the Spanish Massacre grounds.

On the top of the mountain just to the right of the center of the photo is a sharp promenant point jutting out into the blue sky. This is known as the Flatiron, and is sometimes called Battleship Point by the local residents of Apache Junction.

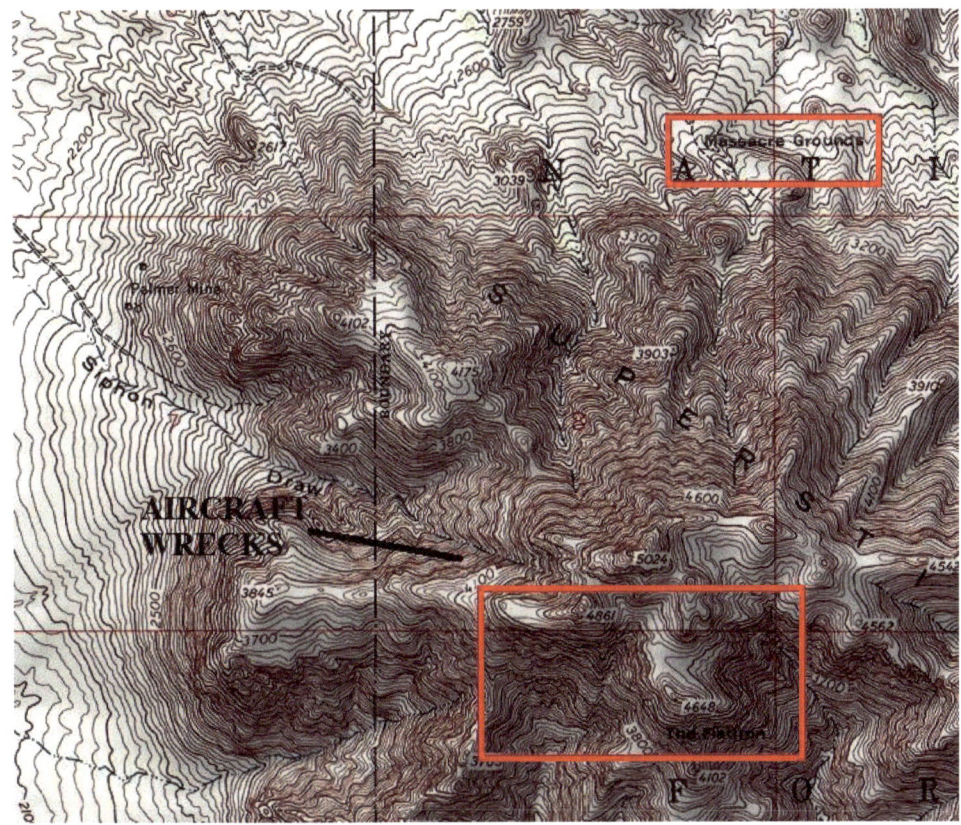

The story of the Spanish Massacre Grounds goes back to the early Lost Dutchman Gold Mine Legend. Simply put, the Mexcian family who worked mines in the area were about to loose their mining rights through the Gadsten Purchase of 1847. This acquisition of land by the US government purchased the lower half of the Arizona Territory from the Mexican Government. This meant the mining rights of the Peralta Family would no longer be recognized.

THE SPANISH MASSACRE GROUNDS

The Family put together one last mining effort which would allow them to collect enough riches to live comfortably for the next few generations. This meant spending a year in the Superstition Mountains collecting the gold.

The Apache Indians did not like the Family violating their sacred mountains of the Thunder Gods, and they set forth a plan to drive the Mexican miners out of the Superstition Moutains. It was a three day running battle which terminated at the massacre grounds. Legend has it, there were only two survivors which were able to make it back to Mexico, and this is how the Dutchman was able to locate the mine.

Battleship Point is well known for the view of the valley and Phoenix for those who are willing to climb the steep trail traveling up through Siphon Draw to the top. In the canyon to the north of Battleship Point is the location of two wrecked aircraft. One plane is the remanents of an old T-38 from Williams AFB, which crashed back in the 1970's. The other aircraft crashed in 2011. Unfortunately, all were killed.

(LEFT) SIPHON DRAW (RIGHT) BATTLESHIP POINT (UPPER RIGHT)

Moving to the east along the south side of Superstition Mountain we come to Hieroglyphic Canyon. This canyon is known for the rock art left by ancient Indians depicting their successful hunts and battles. This place had permenant water and is sacred to the Indians. The Apaches bored holes in the rock to capture the rain water. They are know as Apache Canteens.

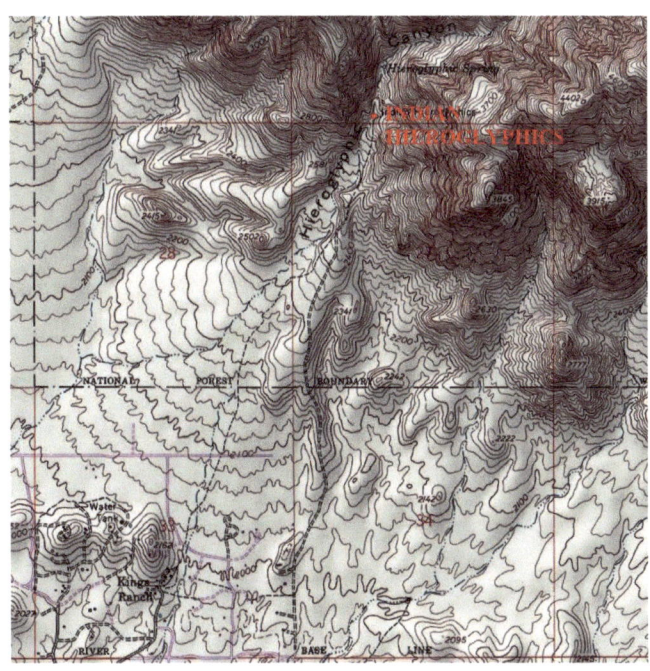

SOME OF THE MANY PICTOGLYPHS IN HIEROGLYPHIC CANYON

The current trail head to Hieroglyphic Canyon is on the east end of Cloud Rd (The purple outlined road just below the National Forest Boundry where it terminates before reaching an old jeep trail). Thi hike is approximately 2 miles. The water at the spring is not fit to drink. Therefore, pack plenty of water.

The next point of interest is the Carney Springs Campground (the trailhead for Boulder Trail), Don's Camp, the Peralta Trail, the Dacite Mine and Geronimo's Cave. Don's Camp is next to t he Peralta trail head, and is used by the Dons as a place for annual story telling, re-enactments of the Dutchman's Story, and trail riding.

The Peralta Trail is the southern route to enter the Supertition mountains.

(LEFT) WEAVER'S NEEDLE AS SEEN FROM FREMONT SADDLE

THE DACITE MINE (NOW A BAT HABITAT)

The Dacite Mine was worked in the early 1900s for mostly composite copper. The shaft goes in about 100 feet, then turns and travels another twenty five feet and opens into a huge room filled with bats. This is a bat sanctuary operated by the Forest Service. If you visit the area please do not enter the shaft or disturb the bats.

GERONIMO'S CAVE (NEAR TO TOP OF THE BLUFF)

THE ENTRANCE TO GERONIMO'S CAVE

INSIDE GERONIMO'S CAVE

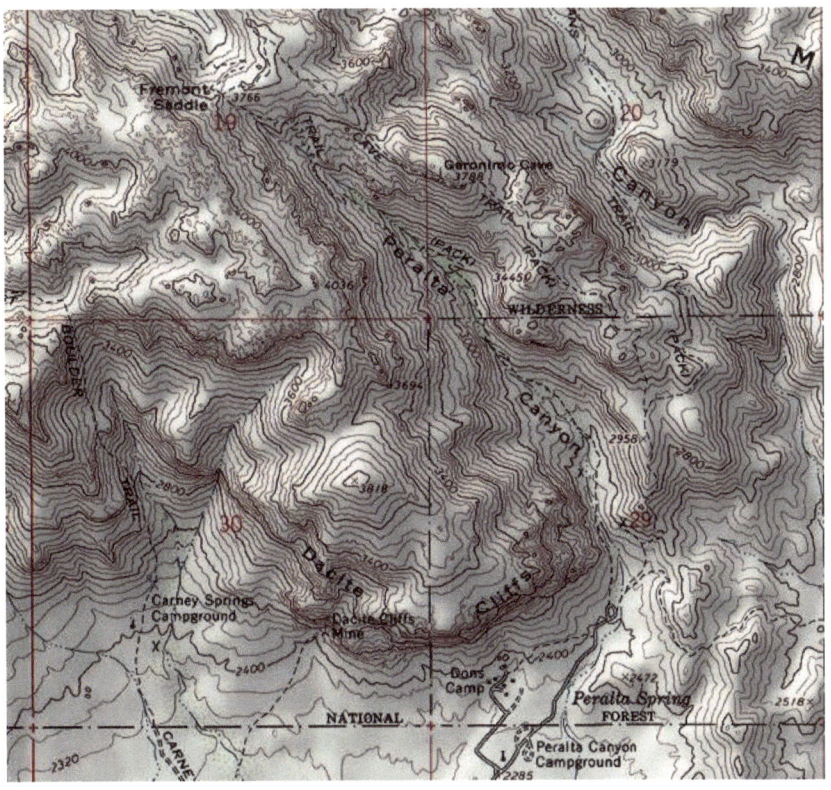

CHAPTER 2: THE WEAVER'S NEEDLE AND BLACKTOP MESA AREA

WEAVER'S NEEDLE AS SEEN FROM BEE LINE HIGHWAY

(LEFT) APACHE GAP (RIGHT) DEAD WOMAN'S CAVE AS SEEN FROM AYLOR'S CAMP

Apache Gap is the passage of the old Apache Trail which led from the valley to the Roosevelt Lake area. It was a perfect ambush point on the old trail.

Dead Woman's Cave was reported to be the resting place of the remains of a woman found in the early 1900's. It is unknown if the woman was from pre-Arizona territory days of if she was from modern times.

AYLOR'S ARCH AS SEEN FROM BOULDER TRAIL

This arch is probably the inspiration to the tale of the moon shining through the hole lining up with Weaver's Needle to point out the Apache Gold or the Lost Dutchman's gold.

BLACK TOP MESA

Blacktop Mesa is probably the most worked areas when searching for the Lost Dutchman's gold mine. This may be due to the location of the Spanish Hieroglyphics located on the south end of the Mountain.

THE SPANISH HIEROGLYPICS ON BLACKTOP MESA

These pictoglyphs are believed by many to be of Spanish origin. Sun symbols usually indicate rich treasures or mines. The ORO is a give-away as to what it is all about. GOLD! Then the map. If you can solve this, you might find the Lost Dutchman's Gold Mine.

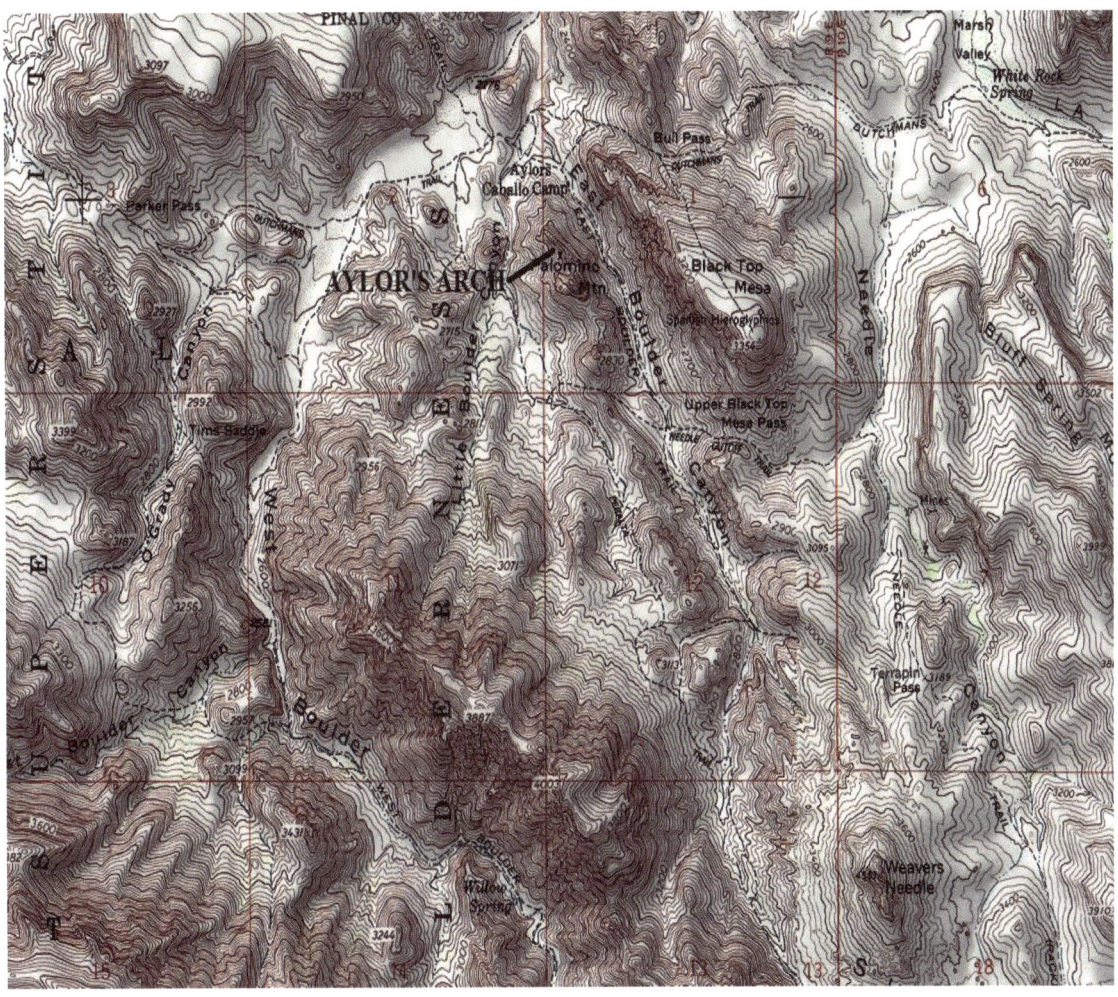

Many events have taken place in this area. Blacktop Mesa and the Spanish Race Track are the places where Adolph Ruth's head and body were found. The bones of the body were located on the northeast side of Blacktop Mesa, and the head was near the Spanish Race track. This event is probably the most famous of the unsolved murders that have happened in the Superstition Mountains. However, there have been many more.

The Author of this book was in a show down with a prospector known as Crazy Jake. Crazy Jake had claimed ownership of the area around the Spanish Hieroglypics. The author was there to take photos and nothing more. However, Crazy Jake accused the Author of jumping his claim. The two were about to draw weapons when an Air Force group came down the trail and broke up the fight. It might be mentioned the Air Force group was part of the Author's group locating the hieroglyphics for a photographic record.

CHAPTER 3: THE MINER'S NEEDLE AREA

MINER'S NEEDLE

(LEFT) CASTLE ROCK ALSO KNOWN AS THE SPANISH GRAVE YARD (RIGHT) HERMAN'S ARCH AS SEEN FROM WHISKY SPRINGS TRAIL AND THE UPPER LA BARGE BOX CANYON TRAIL

HERMAN'S CAVE IN UPPER LA BARGE BOX CANYON

CAVE WITH TWO ROOM HOUSE NEAR WHISKEY SPRING AND LA BARGE CANYON TRAILS

PERALTA MASTER MAP

THE PERALTA MASTER MAP IN CHARLESBOIS CANYON

CHAPTER 4: THE HORSE MESA AND FISH CREEK AREA

**(LEFT) FISH CREEK FALLS ONLY VISIBLE AFTER HARD RAIN
(RIGHT) APACHE LAKE FROM THE TOP OF HORSE MESA**

**(LEFT) PRIEST BLESSING THE CHURCH TREASURE
(RIGHT) THE PRIEST'S ALTER ON HORSE MESA**

The picture of the Priest blessing the Church Treasure is from the Priest Map. This map is one four maps known as the Peralta Stone Maps, and are on display at the Mesa Southwest Meseum, Mesa Arizona. Many believe these maps are the key to finding the Lost Dutchman's Gold Mine because the Dutchman's mine was actually a Spanish mine previously belonging to the Peralta Family.

(LEFT) ARROW CAVE SYMBOL ON THE UPPER TRAIL MAP OF THE PERLATA STONE MAPS   (RIGHT) ARROW CAVE ON HORSE MESA

THE STONE CORRAL ON TOP OF HORSE MESA

MEXICAN CART TRACKS WORN INTO SOLID ROCK ON CORONADO MESA

(LEFT) OLD SPANISH MINE IN FISHCREEK (RIGHT) BUILDING IN CAVE

(LEFT) IS THE APACHE STONE HEAD—OVERLOOKING THE LOST DUTCHMAN'S GOLD MINE? (RIGHT) A SPANISH BANK

A SECOND SPANISH BANK DISCOVERED

SECOND SPANISH BANK ROOF IS COVERED WITH SPIDERS

Explorers check out the second
Spanish bank after clearing the spiders

HORSE MESA AND FISH CREEK AREA

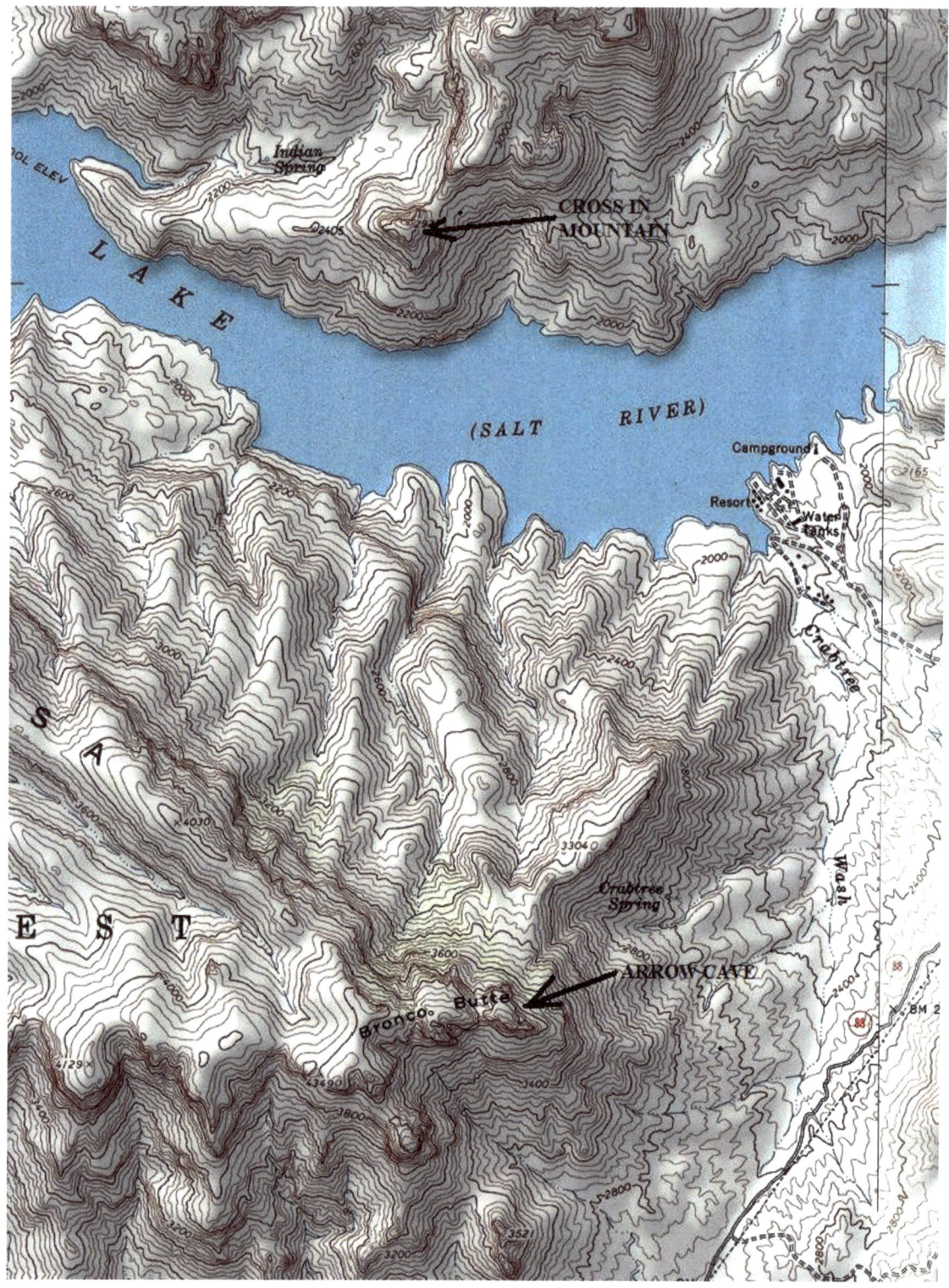

EAST END OF HORSE MESA

THE ANGEL SPRINGS CLIFF DWELLINGS

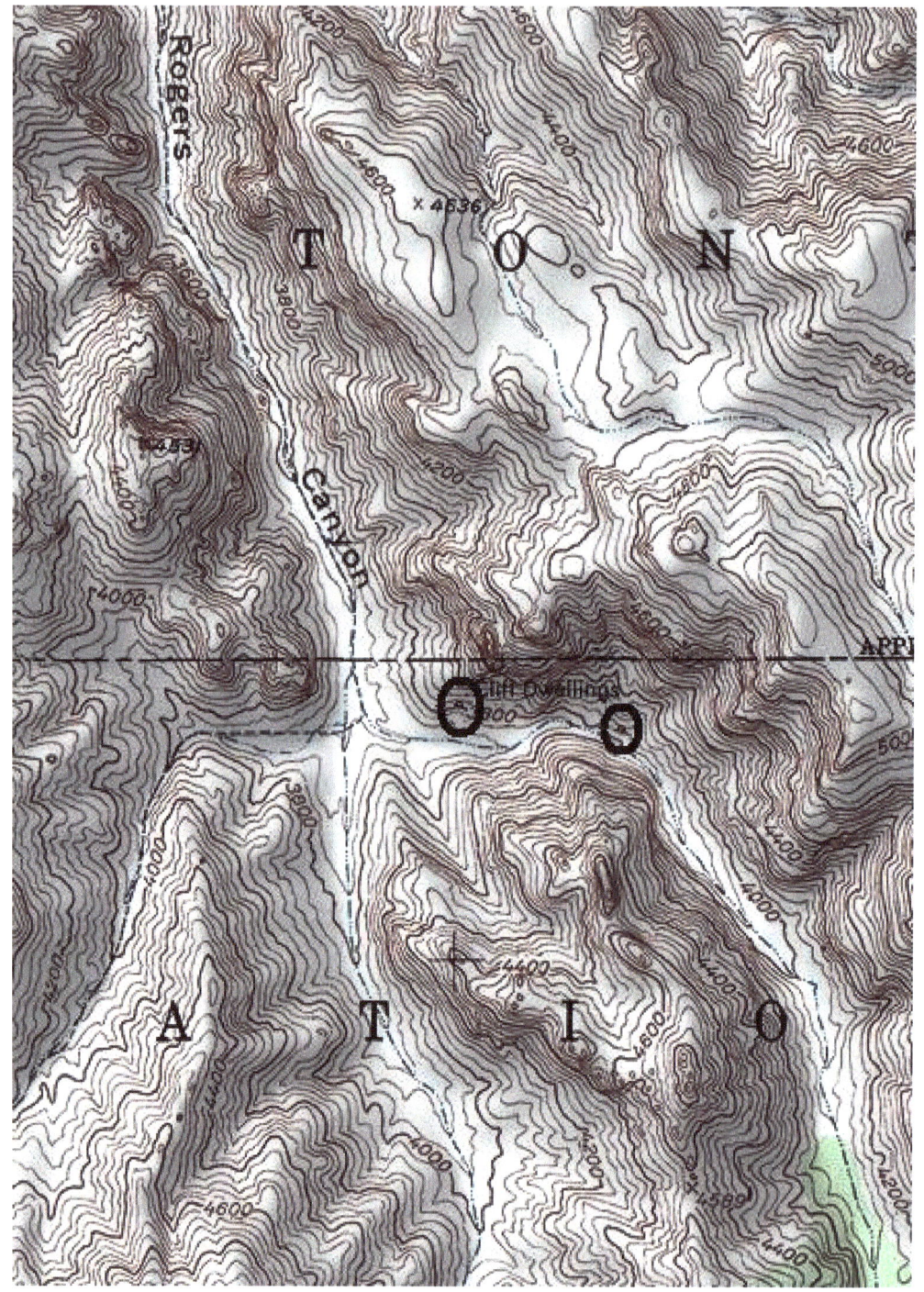

THE ANGEL SPRINGS CLIFF DWELLINGS

CHAPTER 5: MISCELLANEOUS POINTS OF INTEREST

THE CROSS IN THE ROCK AS SEEN FROM THE APACHE LAKE MARINA PARKING LOT

CIRCLESTONE

Circlestone is considered by many to be the Stone Hinge of Arizona. It is a prehistoric structures that has an outer wall structure with a building in the center. There are spokes of rock going from the building in the center to the outer circular walls. Many believe these spokes are to correspond with the four seasons.

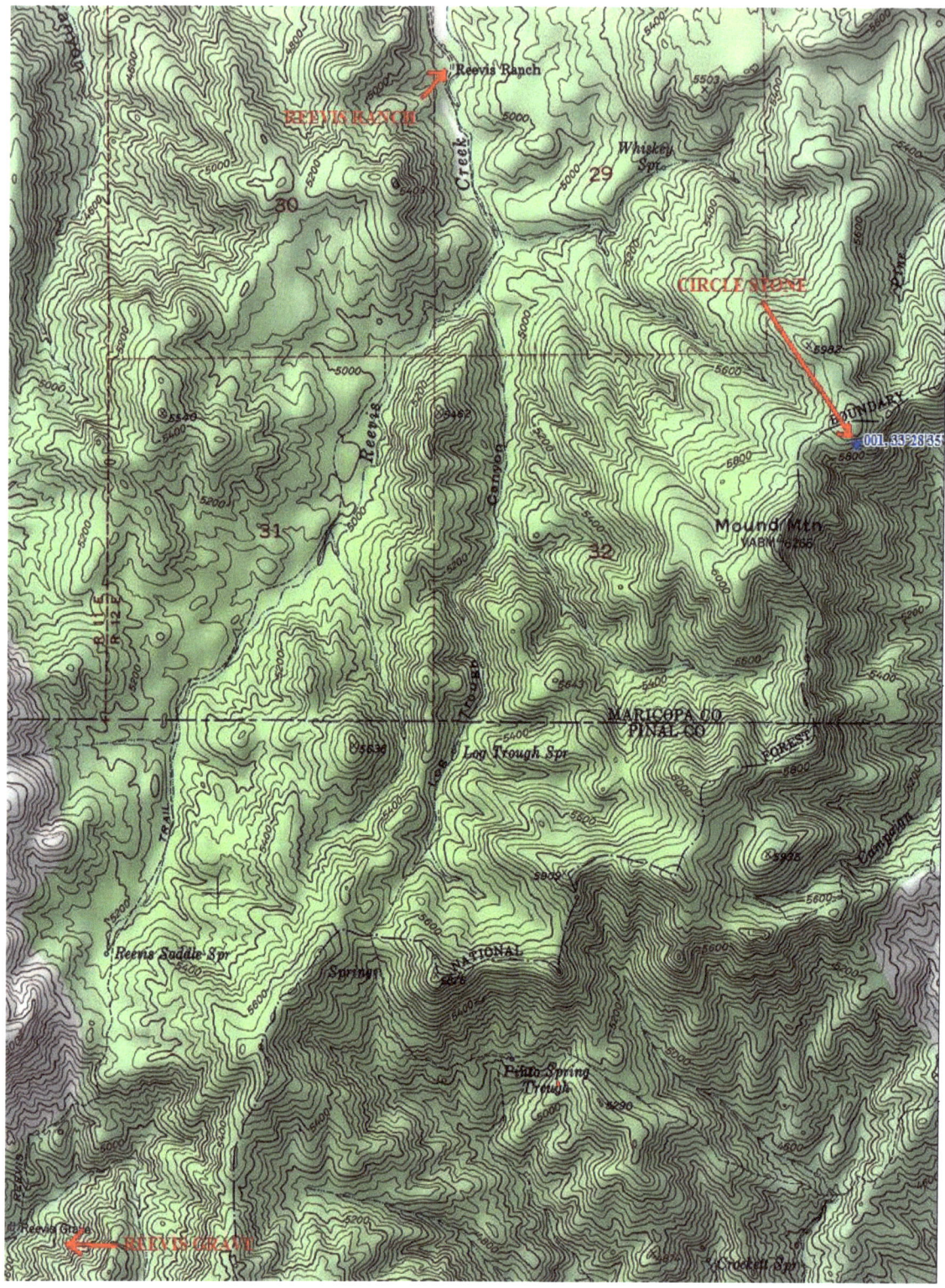

CIRCLE STONE, REEVIS GRAVE, AND REEVIS RANCH

COURSAIR AIRCRAFT WRECKAGE ON MAVERICK MOUNTAIN

The story behind the aircraft wreckage is a tragic one. The weck happened in the 1950's when the flight of three Coarsair F4U4 fighter aircraft left Williams Air Force base. The cloud cover was very low, and the they did not trust their instruments. The first plane hit the mountain ridge and exploded. The other two aircraft circled north back to see what had happened to the wingman. The second plane hit the same ridge on the opposite side of the first. Again, the third turned north and started to gain some altitude, but actually hit another mountain some 5 miles north of the other two. The wreckage sites have been mostly cleaned up, but there are a few smaller parts and pieces left.

ROOSEVELT DAM

ABOUT THE AUTHOR

Mitch Waite is a native-born Arizona cowboy, and he grew up with the Superstition Mountains in his backyard. He knows the Superstition Mountains like no other. His advice to those who want to hike the Superstitions is to remember, these mountains can and do kill those who are unprepared. His favorite quote about the Superstition Mountains came from an unknown, old prosector, "Everything either bites, sticks, stinges, or eats meat."

SOUTHWEST PUBLICATIONS
3836 EAST DEWBERRY AVE
MESA, ARZIONA
85206
EMAIL: GOLD527@AOL.COM

THESE PRODUCTS MAY BE PURCHASED THROUGH AMAZON.COM, BARNES AND
NOBLE, AND SOUTHWEST PUBLICATIONS. THESE PRODUCTS MAY BE ORDERED
THROUGH MOST BOOK STORES AND DISTRIBUTORS VIA THE ISBN SYSTEM.
MOST OF THESE BOOK PRODUCTS ARE AVAILABLE FOR NOOK AND KINDLE.

ATVs, Build Your Own From Scratch, Authored by Mitchell Waite, Designed by Shannon

Waite, List Price: **$12.95** , **8.5" x 11"** (21.59 x 27.94 cm), Full Color on White paper, 46 pages , ISBN-13: 978-1466485112, ISBN-10: 1466485116, BISAC: Transportation / General step-by-step instructions on how to build and assemble an ATV from scratch. Totally illustrated with diagrams and photographs. This ATV also features roll bars and cage for safety. Designed for a top speed of 45 MPH.

Bigfoot in Arizona Documentary, Part 1, Mitchell Waite (Producer), MogollonMonster.com

Productions (Studio), List Price: **$11.95**, **60 minutes,** NTSC, UPC: 886470029396 A chronological sequence of documentary videos of research of the Bigfoot in Arizona known as the Mogollon Monster. Part 1 Mogollon Monster introduction and early expeditions on to the Mogollon Rim of Arizona

Bigfoot In Arizona, Documentary, Part 2 Close Encounters, Mitchell Waite (Director), MogollonMonster.com (Studio)

List Price: **$11.95**, **60 minutes,** NTSC, UPC: 886470301782, The MogollonMonster.com Team takes on a major expedition to learn more about Arizona's Bigfoot. During a night ops event, they run into something that is not happy at them. Later in the night, something comes to their camp.

Bigfoot Research 2009 (DVD) Major Mitchell Waite (Director), MogollonMonster.com Productions (Studio), List Price: **$11.95**, **93 minutes,** NTSC

UPC: 886470563418, Chronological documentation videos of Bigfoot research of the Mogollon Monster, Arizona's Bigfoot. These videos record the progress, findings, events and encounters of the MogollonMonster.com research team on the Mogollon Rim of Arizona.

Bigfoot Shelters And Nests, Mitch Waite (Director), Mogollon Monster Studios (Studio)

List Price: **$11.95**, **93 minutes,** NTSC, UPC: 88647033779,, The MogollonMonster.com team has spent four years compiling data, photos, and video of Bigfoot homes, shelters and hunting blinds. Where do they sleep? What is their social structure like? And Much more.

The Mogollon Monster, Arizona's Bigfoot, Authored by Susan Farnsworth, List Price: $9.95

5" x 8" (12.7 x 20.32 cm), Black & White on White paper, 110 pages, ISBN-13: 978-1461016267
ISBN-10: 1461016266, BISAC: Nature / Wildlife, A collection of campfire stories of the Mogollon Monster, Arizona's Bigfoot as told by the Locals of Northern Arizona

More Mogollon Monster, Arizona's Bigfoot, Authored by Susan Farnsworth, Authored with

Major Mitchell Waite, List Price: **$9.95 5" x 8"** (12.7 x 20.32 cm),, Black & White on White paper, 124 pages, ISBN-13: 978-1468064711, ISBN-10: 1468064711 , BISAC: Nature / Wildlife, Part 1: More tales of the Mogollon Monster, Arizona's Bigfoot compiled from the locals of Northern Arizona. Part 2: Actual Bigfoot field research conducted by MogollonMonster.com

Chasing the Mogollon Monster, Arizona's Bigfoot (DVD), Mitchell Waite (Producer),

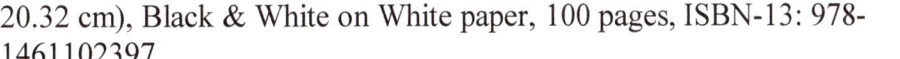

MogollonMonster.com (Studio), The Mogollon Monster Team (Actors), List Price: $9.95
56 minutes, NTSC, UPC: 886470006137, A selection of documentary film clips of Bigfoot researchers chasing the Mogollon Monster, Arizona's Bigfoot. Location is on the Mogollon Rim in Arizona. The team locates footprints, nests, scat, and experiences many vocalizations.

Have You Ever Seen A UFO?, Authored by Susan Farnsworth, List Price: $8.95, 5" x 8" (12.7 x

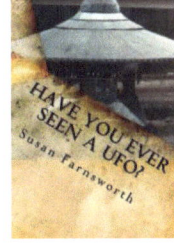

20.32 cm), Black & White on White paper, 100 pages, ISBN-13: 978-1461102397
ISBN-10: 1461102391, BISAC: Social Science / General, A selection of interviews with those who would know about UFOs--Our Military. Was Roswell real? Are there little green men?

The Continuing Search for the Lost Dutchman's Gold Mine Authored by Mitchell Waite, List 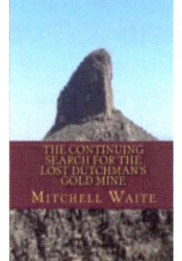 Price: $9.95 5" x 8" (12.7 x 20.32 cm), Black & White on White paper, 152 pages, ISBN-13: 978-1461016229, ISBN-10: 1461016223, BISAC: History / United States / State & Local / Southwest
A study and research of the Lost Dutchman's Gold Mine in the Superstition Mountains of Arizona

Blood, Gold, And The Superstition Mountains, Authored by Mr. Mitchell Waite, List Price: 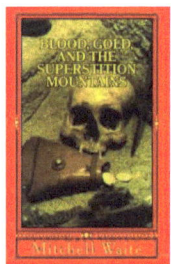 $9.95, 5" x 8" (12.7 x 20.32 cm), Black & White on White paper, 196 pages, ISBN-13: 978-1461096153, ISBN-10: 1461096154, BISAC: Fiction / Historical,, An action/adventure thriller based on the legends and lore of the Lost Dutchman's Gold Mine and the Superstition Mountains of Arizona. Based on real people, places, events and treasure maps.

Blood, Gold, And The Superstition Mountains, The Return, Authored by Mitchell Waite, List  Price: $9.95, 5" x 8" (12.7 x 20.32 cm), Black & White on White paper 134 pages, ISBN-13: 978-1461115502, ISBN-10: 1461115507, BISAC: Fiction / Mystery & Detective / General
An exciting action/thriller adventure story of the Lost Dutchman Gold Mine as it takes place in modern times. Based on history, real people, and events, this fictional novel will keep you glued to your seats till the end.

Gold Panning Equipment, Build Your Own, Authored by Mitchell Waite, List Price: $8.95, 5" 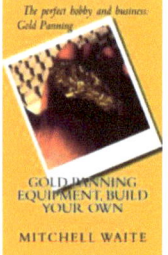 x 8" (12.7 x 20.32 cm), Black & White on White paper 80 pages ISBN-13: 978-1461135951, ISBN-10: 1461135958, BISAC: Crafts & Hobbies / General, Instructions and plans to build effective gold extraction equipment.

READING TREASURE MAP SIGNS AND SYMBOLS, Authored by Mitchell Waite, An in

depth study of reading treasure maps symbol by symbol. The book also proposes solutions for several well known Spanish treasure maps and symbols found in the Superstition Mountains of Arizona. It goes even further and discusses cactus markers for treasure trails in the deserts of the Southwest US and Mexico. List price: $19.95 Paperback: 124 pages, Publisher, CreateSpace (July 1, 2011, Language: English, ISBN-10: 1463685513 ISBN-13: 978-1463685515

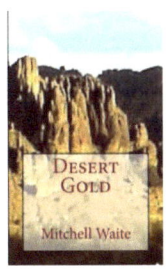
Desert Gold Authored by Major Mitchell Waite, List Price: $9.95, 5" x 8" (12.7 x 20.32 cm) Black & White on White paper, 156 page, ISBN-13: 978-1463777067, ISBN-10: 146377706X
BISAC: Drama / American**,** A tale of love, lost gold, and treachery in the Superstition Mountains of Arizona. A true western novel based on the legends and lore and history of Arizona.

Lost Dutchman Gold Mine Research And Related Stories, Authored by Major Mitchell Waite
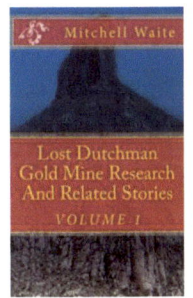
List Price: $14.95, 5" x 8" (12.7 x 20.32 cm) Black & White on White paper, 196 pages ISBN-13: 978-1466230385 ISBN-10: 146623038X, BISAC: History / United States / State & Local / Southwest**,** A unique twist on research for the Lost Dutchman's Gold Mine and the related stories of the Superstition Mountains

The SKS 7.62X39 mm Rifle Disassembly And Cleaning Guide , Authored by Major Mitchell

Waite, List Price: **$9.95, 5.25" x 8"** (13.335 x 20.32 cm), Full Color on White paper, 36 pages, ISBN-13: 978-1468119718, ISBN-10: 1468119710, BISAC: Sports & Recreation / Shooting, Complete disassembly and cleaning instructions for the SKS 7.62mm Rifle.

Esperanza Breathe, Authored by Norma Matheson , List Price: **$9.95**, **5" x 8"** (12.7 x 20.32 cm), Black & White on White paper, 248 pages, ISBN-13: 978-1468091489, ISBN-10: 1468091484 , BISAC: Fiction / Christian / Romance An action packed romance thriller of a young woman's struggle with her drug biological drug cartel family she has never known. They learn of her existence and decide to eliminate her because of her new found FBI friend.

www.ingramcontent.com/pod-product-compliance
Lightning Source LLC
Chambersburg PA
CBHW041519280526
45792CB00004B/1310